CRYSTALS FOR BEGINNERS:

The Ultimate Beginners Guide to Understanding and Using Healing Crystals and Stones

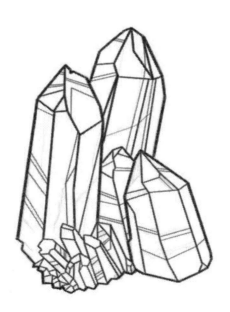

- *Ella Hughes* -

Do you want to connect with other crystal lovers and share knowledge and experiences?

Join **The World of Crystals** on Facebook!

Simply follow this link to join –
http://bit.ly/theworldofcrystals

Or

Search "**The World of Crystals**" in the Facebook search bar.

Also Available in Kindle and Paperback with Colored Images:

https://amzn.to/3cYkhk7

Table of Contents

Introduction

*W*e're made of star stuff, Carl Sagan once said.

To most of us, his famous words might sound like an unrealistic concept, but they become far more believable when you consider the universe around us and how we came to be.

Created and formed through billions of years of celestial events, the Earth is said to contain the essence of the universe. Carbon, oxygen, and nitrogen are the basic building blocks of life on Earth - and these same elements are believed to have come from the explosive formation of stars some 4.5 billion years ago. But the stars left behind more than these basic ingredients of earth and man.

Underneath our planet's rich soil, tucked away in untouched patches of land, water, and vegetation, collected by those who believe in their unparalleled power - crystals are mysterious objects, shedding light on the bond our planet shares with the stars, and serving as our link to the universe around us.

Crystals have been used for thousands of years through almost every culture and in almost every country. These arcane relics are believed to contain the essence of the stars, allowing them to directly affect the human form. So it's no wonder how the once ancient practice of harnessing the benefits of healing crystals has managed to retain its relevance and purpose in modern times.

From health, to mindfulness, to productivity, and protection - healing crystals have made their own niche in our modern day society. These days, crystals are widely available throughout the market, allowing anyone and everyone to access and attain the benefits they promise.

Are you one of many cosmic warriors hoping to make a place for healing crystals in your life?

In this comprehensive beginner's guide to healing crystals, I will be sharing everything you need to know to get started with the practice. Learn about their mysterious origins and how they were first used in early civilizations. Find out how they work, the science behind their benefits, and how you can use them. And ultimately, discover how the often underestimated power of crystals *can turn your life around and improve every facet of your life.*

This guide shares all the information essential to starting a healing crystal practice, and provides insight on specific strategies that work best for *each individual person* - allowing you to create a healing crystal practice that truly suits *what you need in your life.*

Ready to unlock your connection with the vast expanse of the universe?

Dive in, cosmic warrior, and let's get started.

Chapter 1:
The Origin of
Healing Crystals

*W*ay back when modern medicine was a mystery to most civilized cultures, people used herbal remedies, spiritual practices, and crystals and amulets to heal the sick and to protect against potential disease. These methods were considered sacred and true, until science and medicine were modernized and these original practices were branded obsolete.

However, it's important to understand that for thousands of years, *these methods were the only ones that people had - and they worked.* So despite the stigma around them, there remain millions who still patronize these practices today.

These days, healing crystals and the powers they contain have become much more mysterious and enigmatic since they're not as commonly used. But that's not how it's always been - especially when you discover just how widespread their benefits once were.

The Earliest Use of Healing Crystals

The earliest traces of the use of healing crystals are dated as far back as 30,000 years ago. Amber from the Baltics was found as far out as Britain, leading researchers to believe that the crystals were considered of such great value that they reached such vast distances. These ancient relics are suspected to have been used as amulets - protecting their owners from disease and illness.

Similarly, researchers have also found crystals buried with the ancient dead throughout various prehistoric communities. Some of the earliest human fossils were found in tombs and graves that were laced with different stones and crystals, which led researchers to conclude that these early humans believed the stones would protect their dead and guide them in the journey through the afterlife.

Some graves - including those found in Switzerland and Belgium - had crystal beads that were fashioned into bracelets and necklaces, which meant that the practice of adorning the body with healing crystals had already been observed as early as the paleolithic era.

While there are still some questions regarding the reasons *why* ancient man used crystals, their inherent benefits can't be discounted. And this is proven by their continued popularity throughout the earliest human civilizations.

Healing Crystals in Early Civilizations

Evidence strongly suggests that crystals were used throughout all of the earliest human civilizations currently known. From Sumaria, to Egypt, to ancient Greece, and China, healing crystals had a prominent place in ancient communities as one of the major means towards optimal health and well-being.

The earliest literature describing the use of crystals can be found in ancient Sumarian text where the author describes how the mystical stones were used in magical spells. In Egypt, crystals like lapiz lazuli, turquoise, carnelian, emerald, and quartz were embedded into art, armor, and fashioned into jewelry to protect its wearers.

Pharaohs and other high ranking individuals were buried with a single quartz on their forehead, believed to guide them through the afterlife. Lapiz lazuli, which was strongly associated to one of Egypt's prominent sky goddesses, was usually crushed and worn by women of power since it was believed to enhance awareness and insight. Egyptian women who worked as dancers would place a single ruby on the navel since it was believed to increase sexual appeal.

Ancient Greeks also had quite a few uses for crystals. One of the most noteworthy purposes they found for hematite was to crush it and rub it on the bodies of their warriors prior to battle, since it was said that the stone could protect against injury. Amethyst - which translates literally to 'sober' - was believed to help with ancient hangovers.

Towards the east, healing crystals had a more therapeutic use. Early Chinese communities fashioned small crystal tips onto acupuncture needles which was said to help balance out energies in the body. Crystals were also used in

Pranic healing which is practiced even in modern times - some 5,000 years later.

A Sustained Prominence in the Years AD

In the Renaissance, mystic healers continued to harness the energy of crystals and used them for a variety of health conditions. Some literature described how healing crystals were used in medicine and most of the authors including Binghen, Saxo, and Mandeville often cited that the benefits of crystals became much more potent when used alongside herbal healing practices.

During this time, crystals were seen as endowed with *'virtues'* which could be corrupted. Some mystics believed that Adam's original sin caused some gemstones to lose their virtue. Others thought that a crystal's inherent virtue could be lost if used improperly or if handled by a sinner.

In this light, crystals in the Renaissance were used with utmost caution and care. Before their powers were harnessed, stones were cleansed, consecrated, and sanctified – a practice reflected in today's process of cleansing and programming crystals prior to use.

Some crystals in the period of the Renaissance were particularly valuable. One such relic was a gem in the possession of Henry III which was allegedly stolen by his chief jesticular. The gem was said to have been given to the King of Wales – Henry's enemy. This angered Henry, and the jesticular was branded a criminal since the gem he had stolen was considered most powerful, capable of making its wearer invincible.

The Renaissance was a colorful period of learning. So as people grew more and more intelligent in their sciences and arts, many wanted to learn how exactly crystals had an effect on the human form. It was during the Age of Enlightenment that Thomas Nicols started the movement towards more scientific methods of medicine and healing with his *Faithful Lapidary*.

In his iconic text, Nicols described that gems, as inanimate objects, couldn't possess the powers and effects that people originally believed they had. And that's when the interest in crystal healing began to decline.

The Rebirth of Gemstone Use

It took around a century and a half before gemstones would once again find their place as a mainstream form of healing and wellness. In the 80s and 90s, western authors made the use of healing crystals prominent once more, reigniting the public's interest in their mystical power and effects.

Of course these days, the use of crystals is widely considered a pseudoscience. However, their prominence throughout thousands of years of civilization makes it difficult to debunk their inherent, arcane effects. Plus, with the advancement of science and research, it has become possible to back the benefits of crystals with *real, tangible evidence* – a factor that was unfortunately, unavailable in Nicols' time.

Chapter 2: The Science of Magic

*T*he main reason why the use of crystals was widely discontinued was because one man stood to say that there was no *science* behind their function. Unfortunately, during Nicols' time, the technology needed to uncover the truth behind the positive effects of crystals on the human form was unavailable. So it's easy to see why he thought what he thought.

Thanks to modern science however, our understanding of how crystals work has become significantly more detailed, paving the way to a more precise practice that truly taps into the benefits these precious stones offer.

The Power of Order

Turn over every stone, search every ocean, and travel all the world – you can bet that you won't find any other item or object more orderly than crystals. Created with utmost preciseness, crystals are considered to have the *lowest level of entropy* across all existing items – both living and non-living – throughout the Earth.

Each gemstone is formed with accurate measures, boasting symmetry and design unparalleled. This means that crystals can pick up on energies around them, and oscillate or vibrate in response. Because of this capacity to receive and emit frequencies, many of our modern day technologies contain crystals – such as quartz – in order to properly and efficiently function.

What's the relevance of this information? The basic fundamental fact that crystals emit *orderly* frequency makes it plausible that they might be able to disrupt and augment *negative* frequencies. In doing this, crystals are considered to have the power of organizing distortion, allowing a more efficient and appropriate flow of electromagnetic frequencies when used against an object in disarray.

We, as humans, emit and receive electromagnetic energies around us. From the food we eat, to the environments we explore, to the work we perform, and everything in between – everything we come in contact with throughout our daily lives impacts our frequencies and realigns our energies. Now, whether these factors generate *orderly* frequencies or *disarray* is the question.

Unfortunately, since there are no objects quite as low in entropy compared to crystals, many of the activities and objects that affect us day to day typically endow negative energy. This is why we tend to feel stressed, tired, and sapped of energy. In the long run, the constant, daily battle against negative energies can lower our immunity and cause the development of a variety of health conditions.

In fact, many crystal healers believe that *disease* itself is negative frequency which can be altered and perhaps cured through the use of orderly crystals. And the variety of health conditions they can address – from the common cold to cardiovascular disease – is truly staggering.

The Link Between Mind and Body

Mind over matter is more than just a popular mantra for those going through tough situations – it's a potent reminder of how our thoughts can influence our body's condition. In a study conducted in Pakistan, researchers collected information on the effects of healing crystals on different individuals and how their openness to such treatment affected the outcomes they experienced.

Those who said they believed in the power of crystals were met with more positive results, manifesting measurable improvement in their condition. Those who were skeptics were benefited much less from crystal therapy, either retaining their condition prior to the experiment, or showing very little improvement.

What this demonstrates is how *chakras* come into play when it comes to crystal healing methods (which we'll discuss further in later chapters.) Chakras are concentrated centers of spiritual energy distributed through different parts of the body. You can think of them as intersections in our spiritual facet. When these intersections become clogged with traffic, they reduce the flow of energy to other destinations in our system, leading to the development of symptoms like pain, stress, and illness, to name a few.

Obstructions in our chakras can be the result of a variety of insults. These include physical injury, strong emotions, and yes, even our thoughts. So if we allow our thoughts to dwell on negative concepts - such as the inefficacy of crystal healing - we voluntarily block our own chakras.

An Openness to Healing

Lots of different theories and concepts in both mystic healing practices and scientific medicine use the idea of a *holistic* self in order to achieve wellness and optimal health. In the same light, crystal healing methods work best when recipients are *open* to the idea. This reduces the electromagnetic blockage and allows better reception of crystals' benefits.

So before you get started on your new journey to healing, consider these steps to help you achieve utmost openness to the process:

✓ **Engage in a few minutes of mindfulness.** Find a quiet, airy space to sit and get comfortable. It's recommended that you find a place on the floor to reduce physical input from sofas and chairs. Close your eyes and count backwards from 10 to enter the state of mindfulness. Maintain your awareness on the now, and let ideas come as they do. Avoid holding on to a thought for too long - simply acknowledge its presence in your mind and then let it go after several seconds of contemplation.

✓ **Acknowledge your current state**. If you're engaging in crystal healing because of excess stress, tiredness, illness, or disease, accept your current health status and acknowledge that *it's real*. Placing yourself in a vulnerable state makes it easier to accept the need for healing and treatment. This helps skeptical recipients become more receptive to crystal healing, since there really is nothing to lose in the attempt towards optimal health.

✓ **Focus on sounds.** It's hard for skeptics to feel fully accepting of crystal healing, and negative thoughts that intrude during a session can obstruct chakras and cause poor outcomes. To prevent this from happening, consider playing ambient music or sounds to focus on. This can prevent intrusive thoughts from taking up mental bandwidth, making it more likely to reap the total benefits of crystals.

Chapter 3: The Healing Properties of Crystals

*F*rom measurable conditions like the common cold and even cancer, to more abstract issues that involve the emotions and thoughts, healing crystals have been found to address, manage, and even cure a variety of health problems involving both body and mind. While there isn't a single, all-powerful crystal currently known to man, there are a wide spectrum of healing crystals to choose from that address almost any facet of your well-being.

Crystals from A to Z

Aegirine

Color: Grey, black, brown

Physical Benefits: Strengthens immunity, supports cellular memory, reduces injury from different forms of radiation

Emotional Benefits: Lends emotional support and guidance in situations where prejudice might be a problem

Cognitive Benefits: Protects against malicious thoughts or jealousy

Spiritual Benefits: Powerful protection properties, used for karmic dumping, increases psychic intuition

Agnitite

Color: Orange, brown, red, gray

Physical Benefits: Improves cellular health and blood flow, detoxifies all the systems

Emotional Benefits: Works well for children and teens going through mood problems as a result of hormonal changes

Cognitive Benefits: Clears the mind, restores peace of mind, and strengthens the user's sense of purpose

Spiritual Benefits: Encourages vibrational unity by allowing heat to enter through the crown chakra and flow through the rest of the body

Amazonite

Color: Pale blue, light green, white

Physical Benefits: Improves metabolic function, relaxes tensions in the muscles

Emotional Benefits: Negates emotional stress by absorbing it and casting it out of the user

Cognitive Benefits: Balances mental noise, reducing stress and tension in a person's thoughts, providing a calming effect

Spiritual Benefits: Enhances perspectives, allowing a stronger intuition to pick out negative personal qualities to properly remove them from the psyche

Amber

Color: Orange, red, yellow

Physical Benefits: Relieves asthma, respiratory disorders, and seizure disorders

Emotional Benefits: Addresses issues like anxiety, emotional stress, and apprehension, even easing a person experiencing depression

Cognitive Benefits: Restores peace of mind and tranquility, known for its capability to relieve distress in infants

Spiritual Benefits: Protective stone believed to provide substantial defense against the evil eye and other powerful psychic attacks

Amethyst

Color: Purple

Physical Benefits: Relieves hangovers, normalizes blood pressure, strengthens the immune response, and aids the function of the pituitary and pineal glands

Emotional Benefits: Tumbled amethyst stones resonate with low, calming frequencies, also offering benefits for increasing compassion and love

Cognitive Benefits: Promotes more intuitive dreams that improve the wisdom and insight of its user

Spiritual Benefits: Helps balance the crown chakra, allowing users to tap into more divine levels of their aura with fewer obstructions

Ametrine

Color: Purple, yellow

Physical Benefits: Cleanses the blood and other organs of unwanted toxins, relieves headaches, strengthens the immune system

Emotional Benefits: Relieves emotional stress and tension, allowing clarity of mind so that users can make decisions and meditate without emotional distress

Cognitive Benefits: Clears mental noise and blockage to provide freedom of thought, encouraging creativity and assertiveness

Spiritual Benefits: Helps open the third eye chakra

Aquamarine

Color: Blue

Physical Benefits: Addresses ailments concerning the throat, detoxifies and drains the lymphatic system

Emotional Benefits: Promotes freedom of expression, allowing its user to speak their truth more effectively and openly

Cognitive Benefits: Enables the user to explore their mind, tapping into less utilized sections of the brain to unlock new cognitive potential

Spiritual Benefits: Powerful protector, especially during travel. Aggressively deflects negative energy.

Bismuth

Color: Multicolored

Physical Benefits: Improves vitality, giving its user a sense of strength and energy

Emotional Benefits: Relieves feelings of rejection and isolation, sparks the feeling of familiarity when its user crosses paths with a potential partner

Cognitive Benefits: Improves its user's capacity to focus, promotes productivity and better time management

Spiritual Benefits: Enhances a user's capability to visualize their spiritual journey, improving insight on the ideal direction for their spiritual growth

21

Bloodstone

Color: Black, gray, dark red

Physical Benefits: Used in the treatment of leukemia, and for cleansing the blood and body of toxins

Emotional Benefits: Relieves fears and emotional anxiety, promoting healthier social relationships

Cognitive Benefits: Heightens its user's capacity to make sound decisions, and improves creativity

Spiritual Benefits: Believed to help its user achieve a closer connection with nature, in some cases allowing users to control the elements and dispel negative entities

Blue Apatite

Color: Blue

Physical Benefits: Used as a powerful treatment for children and adults suffering from ADHD and ASD

Emotional Benefits: Releases sexual tension by encouraging its user to tap into their sexuality and sense of love without feeling guilt or apprehension

Cognitive Benefits: Clears the mind to allow users to think more freely and generate ideas more easily

Spiritual Benefits: Aligns all the chakras for a consistent and unobstructed flow of energy

Carnelian

Color: Yellow, orange

Physical Benefits: Treats arthritis and disorders concerning the nervous system, helps address impotence

Emotional Benefits: Addresses the feeling of disconnected-ness, letting users achieve more meaningful relationships

Cognitive Benefits: Sharpens concentration and focus, limiting absentmindedness and lack of inspiration

Spiritual Benefits: Anchors its user in the present reality, supporting users in their spiritual journey and providing guidance through clarity of the chakras

Celestine

Color: Pale blue, dark blue, white

Physical Benefits: Dissolves pain and helps relieve discomfort in all of its physical forms

Emotional Benefits: Gentle and calming, this stone imparts tranquility and peacefulness to your relationships and current emotional state

Cognitive Benefits: Used as a guide when making big, significant decisions because of its capabilities of instilling excellent clarity and purpose.

Spiritual Benefits: Said to be an effective stone for contacting angels, works as a compass for those who are spiritually lost

Charoite

Color: Pink, purple

Physical Benefits: Works to strengthen the body, minimizing and controlling the symptoms of disease and illness. It also helps overcome exhaustion by stimulating efficient blood pressure and pulse rate.

Emotional Benefits: Clears emotional distress, and promotes a positive mindset for efficient communication with those around the user

Cognitive Benefits: Encourages seamless communication and expression of thoughts and ideas

Spiritual Benefits: Used to communicate with lost loved ones and those who have crossed to the afterlife. May also help connect its user to higher beings in astral and spiritual realms

Chrysocolla

Color: Green, blue

Physical Benefits: Believed to relieve menstrual pain, hormonal imbalance, ulcers, arthritis, and afflictions involving the lungs and thyroid glands

Emotional Benefits: Alleviates a user's feelings of guilt, fear, and insecurity

Cognitive Benefits: Reinforces ideas of creativity and inventiveness

Spiritual Benefits: Soothes the stresses and injuries of the seven chakras, encouraging the efficient flow of energy through each one

Citrine

Color: Yellow

Physical Benefits: Aids in digestion and other conditions affecting the gastrointestinal system, as well as activates and balances the thyroid and thymus

Emotional Benefits: Raises self-esteem to reduce the chances of self-damaging behavior

Cognitive Benefits: Reinforces the user's capability to take on challenges with ideas of prosperity and success

Spiritual Benefits: Highly intuitive stone can warn its owners prior to a psychic attack. Typically seen as the ideal stone for finance-related intentions

Clear Quartz

Color: Clear

Physical Benefits: Master Healer - used for any and all ailments of the body, emphasizes the benefits of all other crystals to provide more potent benefits

Emotional Benefits: Energizes, cleanses, and restores the emotional facet to remove all negative vibrations and bad energies

Cognitive Benefits: Clear the mind and provide a strong sense of inner peace and true, blissful joy

Spiritual Benefits: Used to cleanse other stones, highly programmable, all-around versatile stone that enhances the effects of other stones around it

Coral

Color: Red, blue

Physical Benefits: Powerful crystal against issues concerning the health of the blood and bones, and works well to strengthen muscle tissue

Emotional Benefits: Promotes emotional growth so users can achieve a higher level of compassion and understanding towards those around them

Cognitive Benefits: Stimulates perseverance and persistence to develop a more stable and efficient work-ethic

Spiritual Benefits: Vibrates at high frequencies, able to harmonize the different chakras

Desert Rose

Color: Brown sand, beige, white

Physical Benefits: Known to help with regeneration of damaged and injured tissues, especially the muscles

Emotional Benefits: Said to address pains of the heart, making it easier for its user to heal after an emotionally draining experience

Cognitive Benefits: Deepens the user's intuition to help in discerning right from wrong, and to help with the decision making process

Spiritual Benefits: Believed to contain angelic entities that help users pinpoint self-made problems that may be blocking them from improving in life

Dolomite

Color: White, sand, beige

Physical Benefits: Strengthens the teeth, bones, and the frame of the body as a whole

Emotional Benefits: Promotes feeling of selflessness to encourage users to share their gifts and time with those around them

Cognitive Benefits: Encourages original thinking, and precise decision making

Spiritual Benefits: Improves the concept of the self, allowing users to elevate into higher planes in their aura

Dumortierite

Color: Blue, black, violet, brown

Physical Benefits: Usually used to treat ailments concerning balance, such as headaches, vertigo, and nausea, as well as cramping, epilepsy, and extreme sensitivity to certain stimulation

Emotional Benefits: Clears away emotional clutter, allowing its user to set free any pent up feelings and let go of former pain and anger

Cognitive Benefits: Improves the user's sense of *here and now*, generates a positive mental attitude to confront reality with the best possible outlook

Spiritual Benefits: Stimulates and encourages us to feel more positive about our reality, clearing away spiritual negativity that might be preventing us from reaching full potential

Emerald

Color: Green

Physical Benefits: Deals with sinusitis, bronchitis, and other afflictions of the respiratory tract. Emerald also helps reduce fevers and body aches and pains

Emotional Benefits: Promotes the user's capability to express unconditional love, tempers strong negative emotions to prevent overreactions

Cognitive Benefits: Enhances a person's mental capacity, promotes intelligence and accurate discernment so that the user doesn't end up making the wrong choice in a variety of situations

Spiritual Benefits: Taps into the heart chakra, and helps users achieve equilibrium between the heart, mind, and body

Fluorite

Color: Green, purple, blue

Physical Benefits: Positively impacts the body as a whole, making it stronger and more resilient against disease and injury. The stone is also said to help relieve the flu

Emotional Benefits: Neutralizes excess emotional energy, promoting more efficient use of energy flowing through the chakras, and decluttering the user's emotional bandwidth

Cognitive Benefits: Harmonizes the thoughts to come up with one, unified goal that's easier for user's to follow and achieve

Spiritual Benefits: Opens the third eye chakra, which in effect improves a person's capability of getting in touch with his or her spiritual side, enhancing psychic communication

Garnet

Color: Red

Physical Benefits: Works to restore health to the circulatory system by cleansing toxins and purifying the blood

Emotional Benefits: Boosts sexual expression, and neutralizes emotional disharmony and chaos

Cognitive Benefits: Sparks imaginative thoughts, promoting creativity and ingeniousness

Spiritual Benefits: Aligns with the base or root chakra to make its user feel more connected to his spiritual foundation

Gaspeite

Color: Green, yellow

Physical Benefits: This stone is believed to help aid in weight loss, optimizing metabolism and reducing cravings to efficiently help users burn away excess fat deposits

Emotional Benefits: Brings feelings of joy and contentment, as well as improving a person's will to mingle and meet new individuals around him or her

Cognitive Benefits: Enhanced perception of reality, making it easier to generate sound decisions even under pressure

Spiritual Benefits: Links to the heart chakra, encouraging a more attuned sense of the spiritual realm and the psychic capabilities of the mind

Healerite

Color: Green

Physical Benefits: Calms nervousness and tension, releasing stress from the muscles and improving respiration

Emotional Benefits: Encourages compassion and love, letting its user establish more meaningful relationships

Cognitive Benefits: Clears the mind of negative vibrations so that its user can think

34

and process information without distractions

Spiritual Benefits: Aligns the heart chakras with the self and mother Earth to give the user a feeling of stability and groundedness

Hematite

Color: Metallic grey

Physical Benefits: Restores and normalizes blood flow and blood pressure, relieves cramps and muscle spasms, eliminate physical tension throughout the body, helps users cease bad habits like smoking, drinking, and overeating

Emotional Benefits: Encourages self-love by reflecting the user's true, inner self, helps us depict our emotional strengths and pitfalls

Cognitive Benefits: Useful during exams, big decisions, and pre-wedding preparations since it clears the mind and makes it easier to decide

Spiritual Benefits: Grounds negative energies and strengthens its user's intuition

Hemimorphite

Color: Blue

Physical Benefits: Used in the treatment for blood related disorders, and helps improve cardiac function

Emotional Benefits: Promotes feelings of happiness and joy, encourages its user to express their emotions more openly, comforts its user in the midst of negative and sad emotions

Cognitive Benefits: Brightens the cognitive plane, making aspects of mentality more easily accessed to its user

Spiritual Benefits: Draws angels near and provides a sense of spiritual well-being and protection.

Iolite

Color: Blue, violet

Physical Benefits: Clears blockages in the throat, aids in healing sore throat, enables users to consume alcoholic beverages without their latent effects

Emotional Benefits: Removes the residual pain left behind by hurtful emotional circumstances such as a breakup or a death, helps its user release emotional baggage and tension to give rise to a feeling of tranquility

Cognitive Benefits: Allows users to externalize their thoughts more readily, also making it easier for its user to acknowledge suppressed ideas and release them in positive forms

Spiritual Benefits: Centers on the throat chakra, balancing the energies of communication and thought to promote the capacity for spiritual discourse

Jasper

Color: Green, red

Physical Benefits: Helps heal physical trauma and injury, and reduces pain and discomfort

Emotional Benefits: Brings feelings of pure joy and happiness, restoring relationships especially family relationships torn by circumstances

Cognitive Benefits: Releases static energy which accumulates during idleness and paralyzes thoughts

Spiritual Benefits: Brings wealth, prosperity, and spiritual joy, grounds negative energies that obstruct spiritual freedom

Jet

Color: Black

Physical Benefits: Protects against illness and disease, providing powerful defenses against a variety of known conditions

Emotional Benefits: Deflects negative emotional energies, protecting its user from potentially harmful emotional encounters

Cognitive Benefits: Maintains focus and concentration, elevates presence of mind to heighten awareness on realities around the user

Spiritual Benefits: Powerful stone of protection used to deflect dark energies and psychic attacks

Kunzite

Color: Green, pale yellow, pink

Physical Benefits: Restores the body at a cellular level, promoting growth and renewal of damaged molecules, balances out hormonal changes during menstruation and pregnancy, and neutralizes stress-induced anxiety attacks

Emotional Benefits: Calms and tranquilizes emotional trauma and stress to produce an air of peace and stillness in the heart

Cognitive Benefits: Heals the mind and promotes positivity of thoughts, removing unwanted thoughts from the conscious planes of cognition

Spiritual Benefits: Creates a protective shield around a person's aura and chakras, preventing damage from psychic attacks

Kyanite

Color: Blue

Physical Benefits: Strengthens the structures of the throat and larynx, resolving issues concerning the respiratory system

Emotional Benefits: Lightens emotional burdens, releasing the user from past arguments in close relationships that might have caused strain

Cognitive Benefits: Heals cognitive burn-out, helping its user bounce back from mentally draining thoughts and ideas

Spiritual Benefits: Works to align the three highest chakras to improve intuition and spiritual wakefulness

Lapis Lazuli

Color: Blue

Physical Benefits: Relieves pain and helps limit the occurrence of migraines and vertigo

Emotional Benefits: Helps make its user feel more connected to our inner truth, encouraging honesty, compassion, and morality

Cognitive Benefits: Assists its user to speak their own truth, making it possible to confront painful realities and accept them to better adjust the self

Spiritual Benefits: Potent protective stone, helps its user understand mysteries in the spiritual plane

Lepidolite

Color: Sand, white, light gray

Physical Benefits: Used as treatment for a variety of mental health conditions, including manic and depressive episodes of Bipolar disorder, anorexia, and all forms of addiction

Emotional Benefits: Restores emotional strength and resilience, making its user feel more empowered against negative emotional energy

Cognitive Benefits: Vibrates to detect negative energy in the mind and dissolves it to provide clarity and peace

Spiritual Benefits: Resonates only with the power of good, ideal for clearing out blockages in the different chakras, especially the throat, third eye, heart, and crown

Moonstone

Color: Translucent white

Physical Benefits: Relieves period pains, cramps, tensions associated with breastfeeding and pregnancy, and a variety of other female-specific conditions

Emotional Benefits: Improves emotional control so that users don't react with tactlessness to situations that might cause them to feel strong emotions

Cognitive Benefits: Said to improve memory and quality of sleep

Spiritual Benefits: Helps users feel more attuned and in sync with their psychic abilities

Obsidian

Color: Black

Physical Benefits: This comfort stone helps users cope with grief, loss, and the pain of separation

Emotional Benefits: Absorbs negative energies that might be paralyzing the flow of emotional energy

Cognitive Benefits: Absorbs mental stress and tension to give rise to a seamless flow of ideas and creativity

Spiritual Benefits: Gives a clear vision of our reality and truth, bringing spiritual pain to light and absorbing it so that the user can operate without astral and spiritual blockage

Pyrite

Color: Metallic gray, black

Physical Benefits: Restores energy in the physical auras to make its user feel vibrant and powerful, improves the circulation of blood, and reinforces the bone structure as well as lung functioning

Emotional Benefits: Shields its user from negative emotional energies, allowing greater insight as to what emotional stimulation a person can let go in order to conserve emotional energy

Cognitive Benefits: Inspires both courage and confidence, providing will-power and self-esteem for confrontations with audiences and crowds, accelerates mental functions to increase productivity

Spiritual Benefits: Fills up the spiritual tank with positive vibrations, ideal for users who might feel tired and worn out after spiritually draining experiences

Rhodonite

Color: Pink, green

Physical Benefits: Restores physical energy that might have been damaged or depleted by strong injury, trauma, or shock, improves hearing and strengthens the structures of the inner ear

Emotional Benefits: Keeps the self-reserved and clam in the face of emotional distress, allowing clarity of mind and tranquility in moments that might often elicit a heightened emotional stress response

Cognitive Benefits: Helps clear the mind and restore sound decision making to prevent ill-choices in dire or desperate times

Spiritual Benefits: Instills a sense of strong independence, grounding its user and helping them feel more attuned to their spiritual side

Rose Quartz

Color: Pink

Physical Benefits: Clears the body of toxins and excess fluids, making it an ideal treatment stone for conditions that result to excessive water retention and edema

Emotional Benefits: Sparks feelings of love and pure bliss, working to open the heart to more tender emotions, and helping its user feel more prepared to engage in a mature romantic relationship. Also helps with heartbreak and heartache

Cognitive Benefits: Gentle, tender, and calming vibrations empty the mind of negative energies paving the way for unobstructed thought and creativity

Spiritual Benefits: Gives clarity and tranquility to the spirit, especially after times of chaos and discord

Ruby

Color: Red

Physical Benefits: Helps improve the health of the lymph glands and system, cleansing away toxins and excess fluids from the body

Emotional Benefits: Safeguards the emotional plane from distress or injury caused by negative vibrations in relationships and social interactions

Cognitive Benefits: Promotes mental concentration and stimulates aggressive focus to keep its user on track to their goal

Spiritual Benefits: Potent protection stone amplifies positive energies around it and effective absorbs and grounds negative energies, especially old residual dark energies that might have been pent up for years

Sapphire

Color: Purple, blue

Physical Benefits: Full body healing repairs and restores different body parts to optimal health, and helps protect against disease and injury

Emotional Benefits: Increases our understanding of the people around us, shielding its user from potential emotional distress

Cognitive Benefits: Stimulates increased wisdom to help its user make proper and appropriate choices even in difficult situations

Spiritual Benefits: The wisdom stone helps enlighten the user as to the state of their spiritual aspect, vibrating at high frequencies to dissolve negative energy throughout the different auras

Smoky Quartz

Color: Brown, gray

Physical Benefits: Heals all forms of illnesses, making it a powerful healing stone in any mystic healer's arsenal

Emotional Benefits: Removes all emotional negativities, making room for more positive emotional experiences and vibrations

Cognitive Benefits: Resonates to create a clear cognition, calming the whole mind and freeing it form all thoughts for the duration of meditation to help give the mind rest from daily thoughts and worries

Spiritual Benefits: Improves our intuition of mystical concepts, allowing users to rise through the spiritual plane and discover more about the self and the world around them

Tektite

Color: Black

Physical Benefits: Accelerates the speed at which its user heals from injury and illness

Emotional Benefits: Balances out emotions to help users get a better understanding of how they feel about certain stimulation, especially those their mind might have chosen to suppress

Cognitive Benefits: Protects knowledge and the sense of reality, preventing the loss of new information to help improve overall intelligence

Spiritual Benefits: Absorbs dark, negative energies exceptionally well, making it a powerful stone of protection and defense

Tiger's Eye

Color: Yellow, brown

Physical Benefits: Helps restore broken bones to proper health and anatomy, imparts impressive strength to allow greater physical capabilities

Emotional Benefits: Eliminates the chances of being overpowered by emotions, calming the user's feelings so they don't act out of the heat of the moment

Cognitive Benefits: Grounds the body in reason and logic to establish more efficient and sound thought patterns for decision making

Spiritual Benefits: Stimulates positive energies to rise through the entire system, pushing away blockage and making way for a free flow of positivity

Topaz

Color: Blue

Physical Benefits: Used as a general healing crystal, ideal for treating a variety of health conditions concerning all the different body systems, especially those concerning the liver and digestive system

Emotional Benefits: Calms strong emotions and brings a sense of peace and tranquility to help clear the smoke that strong feelings might cast over cognition

Cognitive Benefits: Widely praised for its capability of improving wisdom to help its user become more capable of deciding appropriately during complicated situations

Spiritual Benefits: Ideal companion for meditation and mindfulness as it serves to open a direct route to the higher self

Vitalite

Color: Gray

Physical Benefits: Improves the level of energy, providing a sense of overall well-being, especially for people who suffer from anxiety, stress-related disorders, and depression

Emotional Benefits: Breaks negative emotional patterns, helping its user become more efficient when handling strong feelings

Cognitive Benefits: Helps encourage imaginative thoughts and ideas, ideal for users who want to generate new ideas for works and school

Spiritual Benefits: Cleanses the spirit of negative vibrations, releasing them from the system, and making way for a lighter spiritual feeling

Note that this is not an all-inclusive list, and hundreds of other crystals are available in the world around us. Nonetheless, those listed here are suitable beginner stones that can set you off in the right direction as you begin your cosmic journey through in search of your spiritual truth.

Chapter 4: Choosing Your Beginner Crystals

*T*here are thousands of different kinds of crystals, and each one possesses unique powers and benefits that might make it confusing to choose your beginner bundle. The thing about crystals though is that it can be overwhelming to deal with so many different kinds if you're only just starting out. Understanding your immediate needs, buying only those that are essential for you, and building from there are some steps you can take in order to make sure your starter collection provides you just the right versatility.

Which Crystals Should You Start Out With?

One of the basic principles of buying crystals is that you don't necessarily get to choose which ones will suit you - the *crystals* choose you. If you intend to purchase your beginner set from a physical store, avoid looking at any of the stones. This helps eliminate the chance of choosing based on aesthetic which may result to a biased selection.

Instead, close your eyes and feel the stones. What do you sense? Some crystals might feel warm, others calming and cool. The beauty is that you don't need to know what these feelings mean - you simply make choices based on where your cosmic compass takes you. Temperatures, vibrations, and strange sensations have no hierarchy when it comes to crystals. This means that there is *no better choice*. So it's encouraged that you choose those that simply resonate with your spirituality.

Purchasing Crystals Online

Transporting a crystal from the Baltics to Great Britain these days takes nothing more than a few weeks, thanks to the convenience of the internet. Of course, while most of us would prefer to shop for crystals at brick-and-mortars, there are lots of reliable online sources for healing stones. The difficulty is in choosing - especially if you *can't* feel the stones in person.

The fact remains that you don't get to *choose* crystals - they choose you! So how can you maintain that method of narrowing down your options when there's no way you can physically touch a crystal prior to making your purchase? You might want to start with this short quiz (try not to take too long when you answer the questions):

1. What is currently the main focus of your life?
a) Family
b) Career
c) Exploration

2. You're most interested in improving your...
a) Fortune
b) Future
c) Relationships

3. You feel you have a natural talent for...
a) Public relations
b) The sciences

c) The arts

4. In the near future, you'd be most interested in...
a) Starting a family
b) Succeeding in your work
c) Travelling the world

5. Your most prominent problem is...
a) Physical
b) Mental
c) Emotional

If you answered mostly A's: Your efforts are mostly directed towards establishing or supporting a family, or becoming your own, independent unit. People in this particular situation might benefit most from crystals that maximize *energy, calmness, and vitality* as the transition towards or the process of rearing a family or household can be tiring and chaotic.

If you answered mostly B's: Much of your energy is focused on your work and your passion. Healing stones that heighten *productivity, clarity, and creativity* can be exceptionally beneficial to help in your journey towards improved outcomes from your efforts at work.

If you answered mostly C's: You spirit is drawn to exploring yourself and the world around you. You're at a point in your life where your main concern is the present, hoping to make the most of the *now* instead of trying to build a future or dwell on the past. Crystals focused on **attracting love, enhancing fortitude and courage, and improving insight** can be most ideal in trying to maximize what you learn from each new experience.

Of course, this is not a definitive quiz. However it may help you narrow down your choices from thousands to just a few hundreds. Another great way to figure out which healing crystals would be best for you would be to look at images of crystals.

Without reading what they're for, simply pick out a few that you feel resonate best with you. As is customary, avoid thinking about your choices too much, and choose the first one that makes a positive impression on you at a glance. More often than not, your intuition will lead you to the right choice without you even having to exert any cognitive effort.

According to experts, there is no science to choosing the number of crystals you should start out with. If 10 different crystals resonate with your soul, then you can start out with all 10. If you find that only 3 stones make you *feel*, then you can choose to begin with just 3 different crystals. Again, there is no specific method to choosing the best beginner crystals, and everyone will have a different experience. Let your subconscious lead the way.

Is This a Real Crystal?

While there are countless crystal retailers out there who are genuinely interested in providing cosmic warriors with high quality healing stones, there are equally as many unscrupulous sellers who simply capitalize on the rebirth of crystal healing. So as you might already know, there are a few bad crystals out there that might not be able to provide you the benefits they were intended to generate.

So, how can you tell if you've got a bum rock? There are a few markers that you might want to look out for:

Bubbles - Crystals are formed through a variety of processes in the presence of a number of different elements and conditions. In all cases, crystals are formed solid - with no room for air to form bubbles. If you inspect your crystal up close and find small air-filed spheres throughout its density, it's probably made of glass, and not raw, naturally occurring elements.

Unnaturally Rich Colors - Fraudulent sellers will often exaggerate colors to make their crystals look more appealing. Remember, since crystals form in the earth, they're typically tinged with earth tones that might dampen their otherwise bright colors. Crystals that are too richly hued, that seem to not have any trace of earth on any of their facets, and that manifest paint on their base and apex are likely synthetic.

Magnification - In the case of clear crystals, like quartz, you can check for magnification. As a general rule, crystals shouldn't magnify any objects in their background. So if you place a questionable stone on the page of a book and the words are enlarged when you look through the crystal, it's likely made of glass.

Perfect Surfaces - While crystals can be chiseled and shaped to make them look more appealing and aesthetically pleasing, there is no such thing as a perfect crystal. As objects born raw from the earth, even all the buffing and shaping won't be able to clear away inner layers of impurities. So most crystals will have traces of earth, cracks, and discoloration throughout its surfaces. If your crystal looks much too smooth and clear, then it might not be the genuine article.

Melting - Some fraudulent crystals are fashioned from resin material that can look and feel like the real thing, making it difficult to tell if they're genuine. One of the ways to test for resin is by taking a small metal needle and heating it.

Place the needle tip on the surface of your crystal - if it burns and produces soot, it's likely real. If it melts, it's made of resin material that was simply designed to resemble a healing crystal.

Price - Some healing crystals can cost upwards of $200 USD per piece, while others can be as cheap as $1 USD per pound. Keep in mind that the price of crystals varies depending on rarity.

Certain color qualities can also change the value of crystals, with less common variations costing more than their typical counterparts. So if you find a rare crystal being sold at an incredibly low cost, it might be too good to be true.

10 Basic Crystals All Cosmic Warriors Should Have

If you're still having trouble figuring out which crystals you should invest in, there are a few choices that are almost always sure to meet every beginner's needs. These basic crystals are considered essentials, and should be included in any crystal healers kit.

1. Clear Quartz - Considered by many as the Master Healer, crystal quartz is a powerful stone that magnifies the powers of all other crystals. On its own, clear quartz works as a cleansing stone, clearing out negative energies from a person's aura. When used with other stones, it enhances their benefits, providing you more potent outcomes.

2. Amethyst - Described as the psychic powerhouse, amethyst helps attune its user to their psychic powers and spirituality. While it works as a suitable beginner crystal, it's benefits remain relevant even for more advanced crystal healers. Some of its other properties include cleansing negative energies and providing protection.

3. Tiger's Eye - This masculine stone is big on Earthly energy, making it a suitable choice for beginners who want to draw closer to their logical, reasonable, and rational side. Tiger's eye stones are great for employees and workers who want to empower themselves and enhance their motivation.

4. Rose Quartz - The ultimate crystal for emotional healing is the rose quartz. Comforting and calm, this light pink stone heals emotional pain and links to the Heart Chakra to encourage its user to feel greater compassion and love towards others and the self.

5. Hematite - Working against harmful energies, hematite is the ultimate stone for protection. Fondly called the Bouncer, this crystal deflects attacks against your aura, and helps strengthen yours at the same time.

6. Smoky Quartz - This greyish, brownish, semi-clear crystal quartz is believed to reduce negativity. Aside from negative auras and thought patterns, smoke quartz can also provide strong protection against insults to your aura.

7. Citrine - The beauty of the citrine stone is that it doesn't absorb negative energy - it completely dissolves it. For this reason, this crystal has often been considered ideal for restoring stressed family relationships. Citrine is also a powerful prosperity stone, bringing wealth to all facets of its owner's life.

8. Jade - Cool, green jade stones are known for their protective properties, best for travelers. This stone keeps its wearer safe from harm and danger during a long trip, and is also known for its ability to bestow luck upon its owner. Humility and happiness are qualities heavily associated with jade, making its user feel closer to nature.

9. Carnelian - Carnelian - called the Singer Stone - promotes confidence, courage, stamina, and motivation. The stone best for workers and students who want to do more with their time because of its properties against procrastination.

10. Bloodstone - Known for its capacity to improve immunity, the bloodstone is a crystal that maximizes health and wellness in all of its facets. This crystal is excellent when it comes to relieving pain and disease, and is also praised for its capability of purifying toxins from the body.

Using a Dowsing Rod

While the use of a dowsing rod is considered to be a more advanced process, beginners can effectively learn how to use one in order to discover the best stones for their initial practice. Keep in mind though that pendulum dowsing might require a higher level of intuition.

As one of the oldest forms of divination, pendulum dowsing allows us to discover the energy of crystals, guiding us towards the ones that are most attuned to our spirit. Of course, in the process of pendulum dowsing, it's important that you have *the right pendulum* to help guarantee a seamless and effective dowsing experience.

To choose one, simply observe a selection of pendulums. Don't overthink it - your spirit will know what's best for you and will gravitate towards the right choice without you having to exert any cognitive effort. Once you have a pendulum, then you can start using it to choose crystals, among other things.

Steps in Using a Pendulum Dowser for Crystal Selection

1. Clear Your Mind - Before starting any process with crystals, it's important that your mind is clear from possible obstructions. Take a few minutes to focus on your breathing and set your mind to the goal of the dowsing experience.

2. Practice Your Pendulum - Different pendulums vibrate with different intensity and qualities. So what feels like a 'yes' with one pendulum, might feel completely different with another. To attune to your specific pendulum, hold it in your hand and close your eyes. Ask it a question to which you know the answer would be yes. For instance, you might ask if you're male/female, and it will resonate with an energy that communicates yes.

Once you've felt the vibrations of a yes answer, ask it a question whose answer would be no. You should be able to sense a change in the vibration of your pendulum. In doing this, you develop a deeper sensing of your pendulum, thus allowing you to better understand where it wants to guide you.

3. Choose Your Crystals - When using a pendulum dowser to select crystals, simply hold the pendulum over the crystal, or over an image of the crystal if you're buying online, and ask it - *do I need this crystal?* Try not to make suggestions in your mind to influence the answer of the pendulum as this could interfere with its true recommendation. Instead, leave the decision to your pendulum and maintain an open mind.

Chapter 5:
The Beginnings of
Crystal Healing

Now that you have the first few crystals for your healing practice, how do you begin the process? The way by which crystals are used is very systematic and orderly, since it's believed that improper handling can lead to poor or perhaps even harmful outcomes. Following this guide on how to begin using crystals can help guarantee a proper process that doesn't obstruct your spirit and the potent powers of the stones in your hands.

Cleansing Your Crystals

Before using your crystals, it's important that you first cleanse them. This relieves them of negative energies, ensuring that they emit only positive vibrations to benefit your spirit. When do you know when it's time to clean your stones?

There is no specific schedule to follow, and you'll have to figure it out for yourself by feeling your stones. If they no longer resonate with the same power and vibrations that they did when you first held them.

While I elaborate more on crystal cleansing in later chapters, this short guide should start you off on the right path.

1. Sage Smoke - Sage smoke is used in many practices as a cleansing agent. The smoke serves the purpose of an 'energy bath' which neutralizes negative energies in a space, and removes metaphysical 'toxins' along the way. Performing a cleanse with sage smoke entails simply immersing your stones in the agent regularly to maintain their positive energy and to remove any negative energies they might have absorbed in previous healing sessions.

2. Sun and Moon Light - Solar and lunar powers can be absorbed to recharge stones and bring them back to their original configuration. Exposing your stones to either sun or moonlight for at least 4 hours can help restore their energy, cleanse absorbed negativities, and reset previously endowed intentions.

3. Soil - Bringing your crystals back to where they came from can help remove toxins and negative energy from their structure. A 24 hour soil immersion cleans away any bad vibrations, bringing your stones back to their original clarity and cleanliness, ready for use.

4. Clear quartz - As mentioned a few paragraphs back, the clear quartz makes a great beginner crystal because of its versatile use. One of its functions is to cleanse other crystals, which gives it a unique position in your set. A clean clear quartz can be used to recharge other crystals in your arsenal as they vibrate purifying energy that neutralizes negative energy in surrounding stones.

Setting Your Intentions

An 'intention' as its name suggests, is a goal or desired outcome that we bestow upon our use of crystals so that each healing session provides us the benefits we need the most. Remember that each crystal offers a variety of properties. Setting an intention helps magnify the specific properties we want to use.

Intention setting can sound complex and

advanced, but the simple process can be easily mastered by any dedicated beginner. By properly bestowing a goal on your healing, you can make the most of each session.

1. Deciding on an Intention - Of course, the first step to setting an intention is deciding on one. And it's not quite as simple as choosing a random crystal property and then saying that's what you want to reap today. On the contrary, it requires significant reflection in order to uncover the most prominent pain in your life. A few minutes of meditation can help out with this. Remain true to yourself, tap into your spirit, and focus on the real issues, hurt, or insult that your aura might be dealing with. This will work best as an intention for a crystal healing session.

2. Bestowing Your Intention - Now that you have a goal in mind, you can bestow your intention on your crystal. To do this, find a quiet space to sit and hold your chosen crystal in your hand. Feel its vibrations and align your energy with the crystal's. Once you feel you're in sync with your stone, speak your intention calmly and deliberately. You can mention it as many times as you want. Make sure not to lose focus on the energy of your stone while you do this.

3. Position Your Stone - Once the intention has been set, place your stone somewhere where you can readily see or feel it so it can serve as a reminder of your goal. An altar, your pocket, under your pillow, or on your nightstand are some of the best places to position a stone endowed with an intention. Feel free to glance at the stone to realign yourself with your goals any time during the day, and remember to maintain positivity when dealing with your crystal and thoughts of your intentions.

A Few Tips for Proper Intention Setting

Crystal healers who are only just beginning their practice might find it confusing how to phrase an intention. If anything, your intention has to be metaphysical in nature, so try to avoid those that dwell on the tangible and temporal.

For instance, when using citrine for its wealth improving properties, a user might set "winning the lottery" as their intention.

Unfortunately, while crystals can be quite powerful, requesting such temporal, instant, and tangible intentions might not be realistic. Remember, crystals maximize your energy - since the lottery is outside of this scope, it's unlikely to come true.

Instead, you might want to say something like "I hope to achieve financial relief" or "I want to encounter new financial opportunities to grow my wealth."

Another tip for beginners setting intentions for the first time is to remember the importance of cleansing. A stone that has been endowed with an intention will continue to vibrate with these goals until its cleansed. Bestowing a new intention on a stone that hasn't yet been cleaned from previous intention setting can cause discord in its vibrations.

Healing with Crystals

Aligning crystals with your chakras can help reduce blockages in energy, reducing negative obstructions and promoting a seamless flow of energy throughout your body. We're discussing more about chakras in the next chapter, but here are the basic healing methods you can use to maximize the properties of crystals for your health.

1. Placing - Placing stones on your chakras can help facilitate positive vibrations and absorb negative ones. If you're suffering from a specific ailment, placing the proper stone on the problem area can help reduce its symptoms. So if you're experiencing a headache, you might place a pain relieving stone on the area of the head or forehead.

2. Wearing - Wearing a crystal can make it easier to maintain a constant flow of energy between you and your stone. Crystal pendants, amulets, necklaces, bracelets, and other forms of accessories can be worn to fall directly over certain chakras, making them ideal for users who want to reap the benefits of their crystals for longer hours throughout the day.

3. Swinging - Pendulums equipped with crystals on their end can be used to swing crystals over a person's body. What makes it unique is that swinging a crystal will make it easier to understand where imbalances in energy might be, guiding a healer towards a more effective session.

Essentially, a crystal healer will start swinging the pendulum over the person's body, starting from the feet and moving towards the head. The pendulum's swing needs to be balanced on both sides to indicate proper energy distribution and absence of negativity. If the healer finds that the swing becomes unbalanced over a certain area of the body, they will continue to swing over the problem area until the pendulum returns to its balanced motion. The area where imbalance occurs is believed to be the focal point of negativity. Maintaining the focus of the pendulum's swing over the problematic body part can absorb the chaotic vibrations to neutralize the issue.

4. Layouting - A crystal layout is one that involves the use of a variety of stones, designed in a specific pattern over the body. The combined powers of the crystals allow more potent benefits, as each crystal heightens the effect of other stones in the layout. Different patterns address different conditions and it might take quite a bit of study before a user can determine the best possible layout for specific ailments.

Chapter 6:
The Combined
Power of Crystals

As we've learned in previous chapters, some crystals are beneficial when it comes to enhancing the effects of other crystals. With that, it's obvious that users have the option of using stones in combination with one another in order to harness more pronounced benefits. One of the ways you can maximize the power of your precious stones is by way of crystal grids.

What is a Crystal Grid?

A crystal grid is a specialized pattern of stones used by healers in order to combine the powers of crystals and strengthen their capabilities. The patterns are typically geometric, and are designed in a direction that moves towards your desired intention. Once the grid is designed, the user charges it with energy and intention.

Grids can be used for a variety of reasons including healing, protection, mindfulness, prosperity, and everything else in between. In some cases, grids may also make use of templates like a printed piece of paper or a patterned piece of cloth. Templates aren't always necessary, but some grids might need them more than others.

Crystal Shapes

The first step to creating a crystal grid is understanding the relevance and importance of crystal shapes. This is an essential factor in designing a grid because unlike the typical use of single stones, grids harness the energy of sacred geometry. So shapes and patterns play a specific role in the creation of grids. While a crystal will shine with the same properties regardless of its shape, the way it directs energy can change depending on its shape.

1. Point - The powerful crystal point is a deliberate, directive shape that radiates with the same intensity when it's charged and left behind. Most healers endow points with intentions because they continue to emit the same goal outwards into the universe once charged with positive energy. Users can either bestow inward or outward energies on a point, and it will project with significant intensity.

2. Cube - Cubes are sturdy, dependable, and robust, boasting powerful grounding properties that make them ideal for protection - much like a kingdom's wall built with blocks. Placing cubes as the cornerstones of a grid can help the user reap the benefit of reliable protection against a variety of insults.

3. Sphere - Spheres project the same energy in all directions. The energy emitted by spheres can be described as calming and gentle, yet immersive and full. Using these stones in a grid can help bridge gaps in your senses, providing an air of tranquility and wholeness to your practice.

4. Pyramid - The pyramid crystal is best for sending your intention outward into the universe. These crystals can concentrate a specific energy and beam it out into the sky, releasing the energy of your intention into your immediate atmosphere. Pyramids are great for reducing negative energies in a space and consolidating numerous goals into a single powerful beam of energy.

5. Harmonizer - Designed as two cylindrical crystals, harmonizer pairs bring a sense of balance to your practice. Using this specific shape can balance out opposing intentions, allowing a harmonious flow of energy without obstructions.

6. Cluster - Considered one of the most beautiful crystal shapes that occur naturally, clusters are characterized by several different points emerging from a single base. These crystals have high vibration frequencies, since they can send energies out through various exist at each point's tip. Using clusters in your grid can help intensify the properties of other crystals around it, filling your space with high levels of positive energy.

7. Tumbled - Tumbled stones are small, smooth, typically oval shaped stones. They resonate with low frequencies, and direct energies outward. They're ideal for filling in gaps between different stones, allowing users to incorporate fractions of energy where they might be necessary.

Making a Crystal Grid

Some cosmic warriors create crystal grids based purely on intuition. This can be a great practice for beginners since it teaches you to develop a stronger sensing as to what your spirit needs. However, if you want to make sure that your crystal grid can produce the results you want, it's equally acceptable to look at those that have been used in the past by other crystal healers. These grid templates - the crystal equivalent of recipes - are designed with different intentions in mind.

There are a few essentials you should have prepared before you start laying down your grid. These items and necessities will make it possible for you to create a grid that's free from negativity and obstructions.

- ✓ A large enough space to accommodate your grid. Outdoor and indoor spaces are both acceptable, as long as it doesn't feel cramped, heavy, or dark.
- ✓ Your intention written on a small piece of paper.
- ✓ Your crystals. This typically includes a single central stone and several tumbled stones that align with your

chosen intention. If you want to incorporate other shapes though, that's entirely acceptable. Remember - your grid represents what you *need*, so there's no right or wrong way to make one.

✓ A clear quartz point. This particular crystal works to set your intention in motion.

✓ Optional: a grid template or cloth. While it isn't required, beginners can start off with a template to guide proper crystal placement. As you become more experienced, you can stop using the guide.

If you're building a grid based purely on intuition, consider these steps:

1. Decide on an Intention - Your intention will ultimately guide what crystals you need, how they should be placed on the grid, and the size of your grid. Spend a few minutes in silent meditation and try to reflect on the different areas of your life.

Do you want to achieve more at work? Are you hoping for a generalized, full-life tune-up? Do you need help with restoring broken relationships? Have you found yourself in an iffy financial situation? Focusing your awareness of the needs of your soul should make it easier to determine an appropriate intention.

Once you've chosen a specific goal for your healing session, write it down on a piece of paper. Set this aside for later. It will serve as the base for your central stone.

2. Choose Your Stones - Now that you know what you want to set as your ultimate goal, it's time to choose the stones that resonate with that end in mind. If you're trying to create a grid of prosperity, stones like citrine and jade can be suitable choices. A healing grid might typically be composed of amethyst and bloodstone. At this point in the process, you might also want to consider the shapes of your crystals. For energetic grids, points and clusters are good center stones. For more relaxed, tranquil grids, spheres and cylinders are ideal.

3. Cleanse Your Space and Crystals - Negative energies in your space can cause disturbances in the resonance of your crystals. In the same way, crystals that have been previously used to absorb or neutralize negative energy, or those still bestowed with intentions may emit chaotic frequencies in a grid.

Before starting out with the grid itself, cleanse your space with the smoke of burning sage or palo santo. Take your time and let the smoke consume your space to neutralize all energies. Once you feel you're done, sense the aura of the space. If negative energies continue to resonate, you can repeat the process. Keep in mind - there's no rush when creating a grid. Take your time to feel whether all conditions are perfect to guarantee the potency of your crystals' powers.

4. Visualize Your Intention - Once your area is cleared of negative vibrations, calm your mind and visualize your intention. Say it out loud to help focus your energy and commit your mind to the idea of your goal. As you do this, take your tumbled stones - or the stones you decided to use for your grid - and start placing them from the outermost ring of your grid. While placing each stone, make sure that your intention is clear and deliberate in your mind.

5. Place Your Center Stone - When you reach the innermost ring or center of your grid, take out your written intention and place it as the base. Then, take your chosen center stone and place it on top of the written intention. This helps charge all of the stones in the grid with your energy, as opposed to holding each one in your hand and setting the intention one by one.

6. Activate Your Grid - Now that all the different stones for your grid have been laid out, it's time to active them. To do this, take your clear quartz crystal point and start from the outermost ring of your grid. Use the point to draw an invisible line from crystal to crystal, working your way towards the center until you've created a single line that connects all of the stones in your grid. During the entire time, try to make sure your intention is clear in your head. If it helps, you can verbalize your goal to maintain your focus.

You can add other items to your grid including flowers, energy tools, and other crystals to enhance its effects. As with the process of deciding on your grid's main stones, there is no right or wrong when it comes to choosing enhancements for it.

Crystal healers recommend that you leave your grid for no longer than 40 days as the intention and the vibrations of your stones might wane if left for longer than that. Cleanse the stones after the 40 days are up, and if you'd like to, you can set them again in the same arrangement to reap their benefits once again for the next 40 days.

Chapter 7:
The Crash Course in Chakras and Healing Auras

*T*hroughout our bodies are concentrated centers of energy - think of them as spacious intersections in a busy cityscape. Several factors contribute to the seamless flow of traffic - including the stop light, the number of vehicles that pass at a given time, and the presence or absence of obstructions like road works and blockages.

When these intersections are clogged for whatever reason, traffic will pile up and cars will cease to move. As long as the blockage exists, traffic won't be seamless, and drivers will become stressed, angry, and upset, generating a lot of negativity in that area. Roads that have been blocked for too long will often result in drivers choosing to avoid them all together.

In the same light, your *chakras* - or potent centers of energy in your body - require a seamless flow to guarantee balance, calmness, and efficiency. If any blockage arises, energy will cease to flow through theses chakras, and will thus be unable to move on to the next part of your body. As an interconnected vessel, our bodies need the continuous flow of energy - like life giving blood - to maintain balance and order.

There are a variety of factors that can block out your chakras. These include strong negative emotions, stress (both cognitive and physical), and injury, to name a few. Restoring your centers to optimal health and wellness should reduce the blockage and reinvigorate the proper flow of energy throughout your body.

In the practice of crystal healing, there are 7 main chakras that are addressed.

The 7 Main Chakras

The Root Chakra (Muladhara)

Color: Red
Location: Base of the spine, scientifically called the coccyx
Representation: Groundedness, foundation
Possible Afflictions: Issues involving survival such as the basic biological needs and financial concerns
Appropriate Crystals: Jasper, Hematite, Smoky Quartz

The Sacral Chakra (Svadhishana)

Color: Orange
Location: Below the navel, two inches inwards, close to the area of the spine
Representation: Sexuality, creativity, adaptability
Possible Afflictions: Issues involving the pleasure response, the feeling of abundance and well-being

Appropriate Crystals: Amber, Carnelian, Bronzite, Tiger's Eye, Calcite

The Solar Plexus Chakra (Manipura)

Color: Yellow
Location: Pit of the stomach, the location of the solar plexus - a complex ganglia of nerves
Representation: Self-confidence, self-esteem, self-worth
Possible Afflictions: Issues involving personal preconceptions, public relations, and self-value
Appropriate Crystals: Pyrite, Citrine, Yellow Agate

The Heart Chakra (Anahata)

Color: Green
Location: Approximately the center of the chest, a few inches above the heart
Representation: Peace, joy, and love
Possible Afflictions: Issues involving relationships, emotions, threats to our happiness and peace

Appropriate Crystals: Jade, Rose quartz, Rhodochrosite, Aventurine, Amazonite, Malachite

The Throat Chakra (Vishuddha)

Color: Blue
Location: Base of the throat
Representation: Self-expression, communication, and feelings
Possible Afflictions: Issues involving the inability to express feelings and personal truths, dealing with other people's deception
Appropriate Crystals: Turquoise, Lapiz Lazuli, Aquamarine

The Third Eye Chakra (Ajna)

Color: Indigo
Location: The space between the eyebrows
Representation: Intuition, imagination, cognitive abilities, and wisdom
Possible Afflictions: Issues involving sleep, mood, feelings of paranoia, depression, and anxiety

Appropriate Crystals: Amethyst, Fluorite, Lapis Lazuli, Clear Quartz

The Crown Chakra (Sahaswara)

Color: Violet - White
Location: The top of the head
Representation: Connection to spirituality
Possible Afflictions: Issues involving poor, shallow relationships, difficulties exploring new experiences and places, repressed emotions, weak connection with spirituality, and the ego
Appropriate Crystals: Howlite, Selenite, Quartz, Lepidolite, Charoite, Sugilite

Identifying a Blockage in Your Chakra

How can you tell if there's a blockage in your chakra? Moreover, how can you localize a blockage to a specific chakra in your system? Understanding what your chakras are and what they're for should help make it easier for you to determine whether they're under attack.

Blockage to the Root Chakra

Symbolizes: Your base, foundation, and connection to the Earth

Symptoms of blockage: Feeling stuck in a situation; a sense of sluggishness; persistent problems that plague different areas of your life (financial insufficiency, dead end job, long-term problems with close relationships); a feeling of abandonment by family and friends; a feeling of just barely *getting by* in life without a foreseeable end; a feeling of lack of control over your body, your fitness, and your health.

Blockage to the Sacral Chakra

Symbolizes: Your sexuality, creativity, and pleasure response

Symptoms of blockage: Difficulties expressing yourself sexuality; fear of exploring your sexual facet; challenges in tapping into your sensual side; moving from relationship to relationship; struggling to feel comfortable in your own body; inability to believe that others might feel attracted to you as you are.

Blockage to the Solar Plexus Chakra

Symbolizes: Your relationship with yourself, power over your capabilities, self-confidence, self-esteem, and self-worth

Symptoms of Blockage: A feeling of powerlessness over your situation; giving others power over yourself in order to maintain peace in your relationships; difficulty acting on your aspirations and goals since you feel too weak to seize them; difficulty expressing yourself in front of a crowd or audience.

Blockage to the Heart Chakra

Symbolizes: You inner peace, joy, love, and sense of masculinity or femininity

Symptoms of blockage: Constantly pleasing others in order to attain a feeling of being loved; excessively guarding your heart to the point of refusing to let other people in; holding on to feelings of anger and disappointment when others around you fail to meet your expectations of them; challenges in giving too much compassion or too little.

Blockages to the Throat Chakra

Symbolizes: Your capacity to communicate your thoughts, feelings, and emotions. Speaking your truth and asserting in favor of what's best for yourself.

Symptoms of blockage: Fear of telling others what you think or feel; following other people and conforming to the majority in order to avoid bringing your uniqueness to light; feelings of frustration because no one seems to understand how you feel or what you think.

Blockages to the Third Eye Chakra

Symbolizes: Your psychic capabilities, your intuition, and your connection to the psychic plane.

Symptoms of blockage: Feelings of disconnectedness with your intuition; weak intuition; difficulty or inability making decisions for yourself without sound evidence and information to guide you to the right choice; a feeling of frustration at frequently making mistakes with decisions that involve the future.

Blockages to the Crown Chakra

Symbolizes: Your brain functions, divine awareness, belief systems, and cognitive functions and capabilities.

Symptoms of blockage: Feelings of loneliness, insignificance, and meaninglessness; strong attachment or affinity with material possessions; a lack of guidance form any higher being; a general feeling of not being able to maximize the capabilities of your cognition.

Keep in mind that aside from the symptoms listed above, chakras can also be blocked out by disease, illness, and injury. Determining where the blockage is simply depends on where the ailment has struck. For instance, ulcers on the feet can be attributed to the root chakra, while frequent migraines and headaches might be the result of a blockage in the crown chakra.

The 7 Layers of Human Auras

Aside from the chakras - which are concentrated centers of energy - humans are said to have auras. First described by Barbara Brennan, auras are energy fields that can be perceived by gifted healers to determine the underlying issues, problems, and ailments that a person might be experiencing. Everyone has a different aura, affected by their thoughts, personality, circumstances, difficulties, and other factors of their unique lives.

By knowing the color of *your* aura, you can get a better understanding of the kind of healing your life needs on a deeper and more intuitive level.

1. Etheric Body - This is the primary layer of a person's aura, and is the easiest to perceive. This dense layer is the *physical* body which may be obstructed by clothes and other adornments.

2. Emotional Body - This second layer is slightly less dense, but is also perceivable to most by way of posture and expressions. This is the layer of our emotions, where we develop feelings of love for ourselves.

95

3. Mental Body - Another dense layer, the mental body is comprised of memories, thoughts, beliefs, and creativity. This aura can be healed by generating positive thoughts.

4. Astral Body - Starting from the astral body and onwards to the next layers, perception becomes harder. This is because the outer layers resonate at higher frequencies, so they're not as readily observable. This body exists in the astral plane and is made of past memories, our childhood experiences, and remnants of our past-life.

5. Etheric Template - The first layer in the spiritual plane, the etheric template resonates at a high frequency and is comprised of our life purpose and our sense of truth.

6. Celestial Body - This layer corresponds to our relationship with creation, all that is around us, and our love for nature and all it contain.

7. Ketheric Body - The last of seven layers, the ketheric body vibrates at the highest frequency and is most difficult to perceive. This is where we experience divine wisdom and our oneness with the universe around us.

The auras radiate with colors, which can be easily perceived by someone who's attuned to their gift for healing. A lack of colorfulness, or a dull monochromatic aura, might be indicative of a problem or an energy blockage in one or more of the seven chakras.

Training yourself to see auras can help make it easier to determine issues in yourself as well as in other people. In some cases, an understanding of auras can also make it possible to determine the qualities of a person at a glance, so you know whether you'd be a suitable match as friends or romantic partners.

Chapter 8:
Protecting Yourself
With Crystals

*T*he beauty of crystals is that aside from allowing you to heal yourself, they also make it possible to protect yourself all together. The protective properties of crystals make it so that you can avert illness and problems in your life simply by way of harnessing their benefits before any danger or injury strikes the different auras of your body.

Protection Stones vibrate with negative energy that neutralizes negative vibrations that could cause harm to you in the long run. Holding or wearing a protection stone will help it find your potential problem area, and restore positive resonance to eliminate the risk of illness and negativity. When placed in your home or workspace, a protection stone will eliminate negative energy to keep you and those in the space safe from physical and psychic danger.

How to Protect Yourself with Stones

Much like crystal healing, protecting yourself with stones can also be done through a variety of means. Depending on the situation and the type of negative vibes you're sensing, you should make sure you're choosing the best method of protection to maximize the benefits of your practice.

Severing a Negative Energy Cord

As a friend and family member, it is one of our responsibilities to be there and lend a listening ear when one of our loved ones feels down or unhappy. Unfortunately, the process of sharing feelings is one of the many ways that we allow negative vibrations into our lives, especially if we're listening to the heartaches of a person we hold near and dear.

If you're feeling the weight of a loved one's current pain, you may sense negative energy vibrations for a while in your life. These may persist until your loved one's situation changes.

Unfortunately in many cases, problems and dire circumstances can take months or even years to resolve. So as long as your loved one continues to carry that pain, you may continue to feel the weight of the negative energy it brought into your life.

While it's absolutely normal to feel empathy for someone going through a hard time, there's no reason to hold on to pain and negativity especially if it's not yours. This is when you might want to severe a negative energy cord that connects you to the distraught emotions and unhappy situation your loved one is going through. In doing this, you can protect yourself from the possible harm and insult that the energy might cause on your life.

1. Choose a Stone - There are a variety of stones you might want to use to sever a connection, but most cosmic warriors would vouch for the powers of black kyanite - a powerful healing stone that's used to repair tears, gaps, or holes in your aura caused by negative energy. Always remember to cleanse your stones before any healing or protection practice.

2. Cut the Cord - Close your eyes and use your intuition to detect the cord holding down on your body. Use the black kyanite to sever the cord, drawing lines around the different planes of your physical body to cut through what's connecting you to your loved one's negative energy. Repeat the process until you send that the cord has been completely severed.

3. Send Away the Energy - Simply cutting the cord leaves the negative energy floating in your space, causing the atmosphere to feel heavy and dark. One of the ways you can send it away is by cleansing your home with the smoke of sage or palo santo. You may also try to add an intention as you cut the negative energy cord. Saying something like *I release this energy and send it away from my home. I am cleansed and my space is free* can add direction to the negative vibrations so they don't loom in your immediate sphere.

Wearing Protection Stones

Crystal amulets have been used and worn for over 30,000 years. More than just accessories or bodily embellishments, amulets serve the purpose of protection, keeping its wearer safe from a variety of dangers depending on the properties of the stone used for the amulet.

Back in ancient times, amulets were used as protection against witchcraft, magic spells, and other metaphysical dangers that could be used and enacted by powerful mystics. These days however, amulets are used for more passive forms of risk which may be present in a variety of situations.

For instance, an employee working in a high-pressure office environment might feel stressed and anxious all day long. A nagging boss, unfriendly co-workers, and loads of paperwork can make a person feel tired and spent, allowing negative energies to thrive and block chakras. Over time, a person exposed to these elements might feel unhappy, stuck, or simply dissatisfied with his seemingly dead-end job.

Wearing a protective amulet can keep the wearer safe against situations like these. The type of stone you choose will help determine the protection you receive. Make sure to cleanse your stone first, set an intention, and wear it as you confront the circumstances you deem stressful or dangerous.

When you feel weak against the negative energy, find a quiet space, hold your stone, and realign your focus by repeating the intention to yourself. This recharges the stone's energy and strengthens your defense against negative vibes.

Creating a Protection Shield

A protection shield can be made at home, in your office, or in the backroom of your storefront, and works to neutralize negative energy in a space. They work like grids, the only difference is that they use protective stones and work off of a protective intention.

The best crystals for protection are **black tourmaline, black kyanite, black onyx, and pyrite** because they're known for their potent absorbing capabilities, able to detect negative energy and store it away in their expansive programmable memories. These stones are also known to create protective barriers around a space, perfect for deflecting negative energies.

Aside from making grids, you might also want to try placing a protective stone near the entrances of your home to prevent negative energies from making their way inside your space. A piece of black tourmaline placed in a bowl of water and salt can help deflect negativity and keep bad vibrations out.

Chapter 9:
Crystal Care 101

Back in the day, it was believed that the smallest act of mishandling a crystal could corrupt it, endow it with negative energy, and cause it to lose its power. That's why we still practice the process of cleansing crystals up to this day, since they can absorb negative energies and they're *programmable* with different intentions.

If you've just purchased your stones, they may have some residual energy from their previous owner, from the shop they were purchased from, or from the long journey to your doorstep. Whether these energies are good or bad, it's ideal that you properly cleanse your stones prior to use and storage to make sure they don't endow any of the unknown vibrations into your space.

We've discussed how to cleanse your crystals prior to use in a previous chapter. But if you simply want to neutralize them, clear away stranger energies, and make them suitable for storage and future use, you can purify them as soon as they reach your home.

Purifying New Crystals

1. Sea Salt - Salt of the sea absorbs elements around it. By placing your stone in a bowl of water with salt, it's possible to absorb the energies of your new stone, neutralizing it and preparing it for later use. If your stone is brittle or fragile, exposure to moisture might not be the best course of action for purifying. If it's solid though, you can keep it submerged in salt water for up to 24 hours to remove all energies.

2. Running Water - Stones that form in bodies of water, such as along riverbanks and streams, are constantly cleansed by the flow of water which is believed to take away impurities and unwanted vibrations. While holding your stone under running water, try to visualize the impurities being washed away. Hold it in place until you no longer sense any negativity.

3. Crystal Quartz - The reason why crystal quartz is an essential stone is because it's versatile and adaptable. For instance, in the absence of other cleansing agents, you can use a clean clear quarts to purify other stones. Simply place them all together in a single pouch or bag, and the crystal quartz will work to remove the impurities of all other stones.

4. Cleanser - Crystals are born of nature, so it's ideal to clean them through natural means. However, for fragile gems that might not be suitable for exposure to moisture, the use of a crystal cleanser might be more ideal.

Programming A New Stone

There are lots of different places where you might find a crystal for sale. Unfortunately, some of these sources might not be able to provide a detailed explanation of where their gem stones come from. If they were previously owned and used for bad or negative intentions, they can cause discord in your home even after they've been cleansed.

Programming your new stone with positive energy and purpose will help guarantee positive outcomes. To program your new stone, cleanse it, hold it in your hands, close your eyes, and try to radiate positive energy. As you do this, dedicate your new stone to good forces. You can say something like, *I dedicate this crystal to positivity and the highest divinity. May this stone produce nothing but love, light, and positive vibrations.*

Storing Crystals

The way you store your crystals is also important, since it helps guarantee that they won't be exposed to dangerous energies while they're not in use. This also keeps them protected against mechanical damage, such as cracks and breakage due to poor storage.

When they're not in use, consider keeping your crystals in a safe, dark piece of cloth to prevent them from absorbing any energies around them. This temporarily 'blinds' them, keeping them safe from unwanted vibrations. A small silk pouch or purse can be a good choice. You might also want to keep a clear quartz in the bag with them to keep them constantly cleansed.

Conclusion: We're Made of Star Stuff

*D*iving into the world of mystical crystal healing and how it connects our spirit to the universe brings Carl Sagan's famous words into a brand new light. He didn't simply mean that *we're made from the same thing that stars are,* but was instead expressing something far deeper than that.

What Sagan really wanted to say was that we're *connected to the world around us and the universe above us.* Our bodies - sacred, mystical vessels full of magic and mysticism - are fueled and powered by the same energies that rush through the Earth and the stars, allowing us to change our lives, improve our situations, and confront all circumstances with the use of the stones that the stars left behind when the world was first formed.

Crystal healing is an intricate practice that gives rise to a variety of natural healing and treatment methods that are only accessible to those who truly believe. Are you one of them, cosmic warrior?

I hope that you learned a thing or two about the intricacies of crystal healing and how it can benefit you, your life, your relationships, and your reality. Remember to use the information in this book only for good, and to submit yourself to the positivity of the universe with each healing session.

This way, you can harness the powers of the stars and all of nature around you, bringing you to newer heights in all aspects of your life, and revealing new truths and strengths that can help you meet the height of your spiritual, physical, emotional, and cognitive potential.

Ps. If you enjoyed this book, please leave a review!

Also, don't forget to join "The World of Crystals" Facebook page!

Join "The World of Crystals" here – **http://bit.ly/theworldofcrystals**.

Made in the USA
Coppell, TX
14 December 2020

45309452R00070